UP THE STAIRCASE BACKWARDS

LUCILLE LAVENDER

Illustrated by Dean McElhattan

ACCENT BOOKS
Denver, Colorado

MEMBER OF
EVANGELICAL CHRISTIAN
PUBLISHERS ASSOCIATION

First Printing, July 1978
Second Printing, September 1978
Third Printing, December 1978

ACCENT BOOKS
A division of Accent-B/P Publications, Inc.
12100 W. Sixth Avenue
P.O. Box 15337
Denver, Colorado 80215

Copyright © 1978 Lucille Lavender
Printed in the United States of America

Library of Congress Catalog Card Number: 77-93248

ISBN 0-916406-96-2

DEDICATION

**For Everyone
Who, at One Time or Another,
In Sickness or in Health,
Can Use Some Inspiration
and Chuckles**

ACKNOWLEDGEMENTS

I want to express my deepest thanks and appreciation to all who made my castaway life bearable, because often I was a bear. Especially to Jodi, Jeff and Julie—my three obstreperous kids.

CONTENTS

Marked: Fragile!

All my life I have envied delicate, graceful, petite, ultrafeminine females. I derive from immigrant peasant stock and, although not large, have regarded myself as sturdy, strong, and healthy as a heifer. This all has now changed. Thanks to my broken leg. I have a brand new self-image.

During an office visit recently, my doctor had some interesting observations. "After extended study of your X-rays," he intoned, "I've discovered your leg bones are extremely small." (Of course he didn't say *leg bones*—the words he used were much more impressive!) "In fact, the tibia is no larger in circumference than a pencil. I think skiing days are over for you. *You're TOO FRAGILE!*"

Did this announcement bother me? Did I, like Bunyan's Pilgrim, sink into a Slough of Despond? Did I cry my eyes out because I had "narrow marrow"? Heavens, no! A long hoped-for dream of a lifetime had been realized.

Now, when the children's father addresses me with a Deeaarrrrr (not the I-love-you kind, but the I-am-upset-with-you kind), I am prepared! I draw myself up to a tall five foot four and a half, while all of his six-foot-two self looms menacingly over me, and with a courage I never had before, I deftly defy him.

"Remember, darling . . . I'm F-R-A-G-I-L-E!"

Disaster to Plaster

The door swung open with a thud. The click of the light switch took on the proportion of a tree snapping in a sleeping forest. There was the harsh, brittle sound of ice sloshing against the metal decanter. Begrudgingly I roused from a deep sleep and pulled myself up on tender elbows, rubbed raw from too-septic sheets.

Right on time—5:30 A.M. An urgent need to kick the smug container of ice water off its perch overwhelmed me. I made a move in that direction, but fell back on my pillow with a moan as the full force of my situation registered on groggy brain cells. A ton of dazzling white Plaster stared back at me from my right leg, the appendage intended to administer the fatal blow to the ice water.

Though it was black as midnight outside, all kinds of noises echoed down the hall and ended any possibility of further sleep. 5:30 A.M. was also the time for the Changing of the Guard.

The smell of coffee seduced my nostrils, and, like a queen in her castle, I buzzed the buzzer impatiently and demanded some coffee posthaste. One of the "guard" in white uniform appeared, and brusquely informed me there was no coffee for patients—or queens—until breakfast. Two whole hours away! That brought me out of my reigning reverie.

I moped for a moat around my castle-prison so that

anyone who came near would fall in and leave me alone.

I opened my mouth to mutter Something Suitable to my mood, when the next aggravatingly reliable intruder marched in and stuck a thermometer into the cavity. I felt like an impudent, chastened baby bird getting a worm from its omnipresent mother.

The thermometer prevented me from saying something I shouldn't have said because I was awake enough now to Remember. I was a breed of "homo sapienne" taught out of a great Book that kind words are like honey, and I must always be a Lady! So—like it or not, a lady I must be.

However, that did not stop me from thinking a few properly descriptive expressions, and a lot of other thoughts, as I lay there sulkily recounting the series of events which had gotten me into this Predicament.

Togetherness

Several winters ago my husband and I were caught up by the prevalent slogan, "The family that plays together stays together." Endeavoring to realize this worthy goal, we considered various types of hobbies and recreational activities. More and more the possibilities of snow-skiing took hold. There were several reasons for this.

We love the mountains with all their majestic beauty and serenity. Trees to us are living creatures, as they were to the man Jesus healed of his blindness. A friend of ours built a beautiful home around a magnificent tree. A long time ago the Creator built a world around a Tree—the Tree of Life. After *that*, He made a man.

Almost human, trees should be treated as such. In fact, the Head of the House has such a Thing against cutting or trimming anything remotely resembling a tree that our back yard is a domestic jungle.

Another reason for turning to skiing was the glowing praise of ardent worshippers who disappeared for long weekends to pay it homage. Skiing offered scenery, clean air, thrills, and was undoubtedly easy as apple pie. Or so it looked on TV.

Perhaps the most weighty reason for my eagerness and vulnerability goes back to childhood. While still very young I discovered my talents did not lie along athletic lines. When it came to "choosing up sides," I was usually left over, and still remember the team captain's painful expression as he or she *had* to choose me with teacher standing over us.

Maybe that's when I began storing within me the will to take a whack at anything. Who knows, I might turn up an untapped talent sometime. Most of all, I guess, I still harbored the hope of someday being chosen first by somebody, somewhere. Well . . . I could hope for next to the last.

So we planned and prepared for our new venture. We set aside a week in December for our historic attempt at togetherness, and then shopped for the necessary gear, from underwear to sun goggles. (Hubby never does anything halfway. Before we were to go on a three-day camping trip some years ago, he came home with enough equipment for an army division. I am fearful every time he goes to the supermarket. He once brought home twelve cans of chopped olives because they were on sale. Seven years later when we moved to another city, I still had eleven of them.) This time he was content to *rent* skis, boots, and poles. I appreciated his restraint, for, as it turned out, we wouldn't be needing them again for a long time.

Elemental, Essential and Overlooked

When, at long last, we were settled in at a famous ski mecca, we used the sensible approach. Daily lessons. As the week progressed, we became somewhat proficient in the basic skills of climbing the bunny slope sideways, snowplowing, crisscrossing, falling down and standing up.

I sorta think King David must have taken up skiing at one time or another 'cause he told the Lord about his downsittings and uprisings. About how the Lord charted his course and resting places, and was familiar with all his paths. And how the Lord understood his thoughts from far away. All this would seem to indicate that he wasn't so hot at skiing either, and everybody, including the Lord, was keeping his distance!

We were also thoroughly indoctrinated in the importance of covering up our Sitzmark (the mark you make when you Sitz down) to protect other skiers, as well as all other beginner techniques. That is, almost all.

Naturally, my big, strong husband progressed more rapidly than I. Soon he was off for bigger, better and snowier "green pastures," while I stayed on the bunny slope. I worked diligently on snowplows in slowmotion (I'm the cautious type), but became discouraged when my right ski repeatedly came off each time I fell, which was often.

Now, one elementary detail had been overlooked

by the expert who rented us our equipment, and by the cute little Norwegian instructress at the resort. It was one of those obvious rudimentary points about skiing which everyone with any sense at all knows intuitively. Everyone. . .except me! It is better for the ski to come *off* when you fall than for it to stay on.

Frustrated by numerous and precarious walks down the hill, balancing unwieldy skis on my shoulder as I dodged veteran skiers whizzing by, I was ready to call it a day. At that moment, from out of the swarm of people who covered the mountainside like ants, my already well-seasoned skiing spouse appeared. Noting my discouragement, he offered a suggestion.

Why didn't I go into the ski shop and have the attendant tighten the bindings? So that's what I did, and that's what the man in the ski shop did.

"It won't come off now!" he said emphatically. Maybe he didn't know, either, that skis should come off when you fall.

This, however, was the least of my worries as I caught the next tow bar and climbed to exhilarating heights. I was enthralled with my accomplishments on skis, and convinced that I had finally uncovered latent Olympic abilities.

I'm flying down Your mountains, God. Aren't they beautiful and exciting! How did You form them? I remember they are the work of Your hands. Was it anything like the way I make bread? Did You mold and knead and shape them? In summer, You decorate them with layers of green, and in winter You frost them with icing of dazzling white.

In Your Book, there is much about mountains. They brought happiness to a young tenor named David. He sang his songs, called Psalms, to You. He sang about lifting his eyes to the hills so he would be reminded Who had made them.

From the top of a mountain You used a fellow named Moses to write down some lesson plans on how Your children could live together harmoniously. Mountains protected them from their enemies. Your children were also reminded of their disobedience when the mountains belched fourth thunder and smoke from storms and volcanoes. And, in return, Your children built altars on the highest hills to repent and be closer to You.

Wow—they're great. How I love You and Your mountains, and Your frosting.

Disconnected from the Ankle Bone

Pleased with myself, and contemplating where I would place the Gold Cup I would bring home someday, I started down the mountain. To set the record straight, I *know* that Pride does not go before a fall. It goes before destruction, and Over-Confidence goes before a f-a-l-l. . . .

Not far from the top, my Career was brought abruptly to an end. Going at what to me was a terrific clip, I couldn't negotiate a snowplow turn, panicked, and threw myself down. The ski made a huge arc. As the attendant in the ski shop had predicted, it didn't come off. Something had to give. It was my leg—with a terrific twist.

In the moments that followed, there was the electric shock of pain, an anguished cry for help, the flashing of unrelated thoughts across my mind—"Oh, God, what has happened? The pain is gone. Just a bad sprain. My leg can't be — broken. I'll lift it. No, I'm afraid. You can't let this happen, God. My term paper. Now I can't finish it. I need that degree to help get the kids through school.

"The kids! They need me. My husband. The pressures on him are already so great with hundreds of people relying on him for comfort and assurance. I can't be a drag on him.

"I won't walk again. The house will need cleaning when I get home, and the dog needs her shots. I can't pull a thing like this. . . ."

Numbness—limbo—unreality—stillness.

And out of the stillness a Voice, "I didn't wish this for you. But it happened, and you can't handle it by yourself. In quietness and trust will be your strength." Through the cold, white stillness came that Presence I knew to be the Instructor whose guidance would become so important in the ensuing months, as together He and I would traverse many slippery slopes. Fortunately, in the lessons He was to teach, *no* instructions were omitted.

Someplace I read an article which stated that, with the spreading popularity of all kinds of new ski equipment, and higher, more rigid boots, orthopedists were reporting an increase in "boot top" fractures. These are more spectacular, and much more serious than common, simple, ho-hum, little ole breaks. When *I* do something, I like to do it up right, so I went for the Boot Top.

Upon seeing the X-rays, our doctor told us he had hoped for a nice, clean break, but this was a goodie with a fancy name—Spiral! Both bones were fractured, with lots of little funny-shaped pieces needing to be put together like a jigsaw puzzle.

Later, a friend, hearing of my mishap, sent me a ski magazine with a clearly-marked article she wanted me to read: "Eleven Common Breaks in Skiing, and Eleven Ways to Fall to Get Them." As I went through the list, studying the X-ray examples of each, I concluded My Spiral was more spectacular than any of those. I thought it best not to try for the others.

Basket Case

Our first few days at the resort I noticed specially uniformed skiers coming down the mountain with long, covered baskets. They looked like papoose carriers on sleds. I learned to my dismay there were *people* in those baskets. Not Indian babies, or, as I had earlier imagined, camping supplies for adventurers on a wilderness backpack. Furthermore, these people were all injured.

Watching these baskets brought down all day long, day after day, soon made me as nonchalant to their plight as were the other still upright skiers.

"Poor fellow," I thought as I saw them pass on my way to yet another tow ride up the slope.

Now, it was my turn to be a "papoose" and to try out the basket. The uniformed skiers, I learned then, were members of the Ski Patrol. Their job was to rescue people like me. One of them appeared in record time. Boy! Was he a welcome sight!

But he didn't know how to fib very well. I had lifted my leg before he came, but not all of it lifted together. Hesitantly, and ever so quietly, I asked him, hoping he wouldn't hear, "Is it broken?"

"Naw," he bluffed, carefully avoiding my red-cheeked, dirt-streaked face. "Prob'ly just a good sprain."

But we both knew better.

He was most expert and gentle as he taped my leg

into a cardboard splint, lifted me into the woven limousine, and prepared to take me off the mountain. After all, he'd had lots of experience with Basket Cases.

As he covered me from toe to top of head, I asked why he had to cover my face.

"To keep out the snow," he explained. I still am highly suspicious, though, that the real reason was to keep me from seeing where I was — high on the mountain—in relationship to where I had to go— way down there to the Valley of those skiing ants.

My mountaintop experience is over and I am descending into the Valley. Dear God, I don't know what awaits me there, but I suspect I am going to be there for quite a stay. And there will be more than one valley.

There will be darkness in the valley before there is light on the mountaintop. There will be erosion from storms, avalanches, rocks and mud washed down from the heights. There will be vulnerability and despair " 'cause there's no hidin' place down there."

But there will be shelter There will be protection from furious winds, and springs to refresh. And there will be life and growth which is impossible on the peaks.

From the top, one only looks down into the valley. But from the valley, one can only look up.

Cover That Sitzmark!

The first aid receiving ward at the lodge was huge, housing about twenty beds. There were several of us Basket Cases ready to use them. As I lay waiting, not yet comprehending all that had happened, the first-aid attendant tried to get my mind off myself by describing his Basket Business.

It seems that some 20,000 skiers come to this resort each season. Out of that number, "only" ten percent, or 2,000, sustain some type of injury. Ten percent of this ten percent break bones. And those are the statistics at *one* ski resort.

Sometime after my accident, I read the cover article in *Time* magazine about skiing and broken-up people like me. It stated that the previous year in the United States there were more than 105,000 skiing accidents reported. Probably twice as many went unreported for reasons of pride. Glad I wasn't the proud type! How else could I get so much attention?

The writer went on to say that the chances for a beginner incurring an injury serious enough to need medical attention are one in a hundred every time the skier goes skiing. After a week of instruction, the figure drops to one in 200. Lessons didn't change *my* percentages, as I thought about all those "D's" in high school P.E. class.

Housewives account for "only" 11% of accidents, while students are involved in three quarters of all accidents. They get more daring and boastful, and push themselves too far. I suppose it's because they get too smart-aleck and show off for all the guys and girls out shopping the slopes.

This lesson in mathematics didn't do much to cheer me. Nor did it help my deflated ego to find out I was a mere "only." I thought I had done a pretty good job of breaking my bones, and had rightfully earned my Place in the Snow.

After being properly registered as another statistic under the heading, "Bad Break Basket Case," I was transported to a clinic in a small village several miles away. Everyone there was nice to me. The doctor and nurse both assured me I would be back. I'm still not sure whether they meant back on the X-ray table, or practicing snowplows again. The doctor told me he and his wife both had broken bones from skiing, and always went back for more (skiing or broken bones?). Maybe that was just sales talk to stimulate the X-ray business, although it seemed to be doing all right on its own.

Gently they removed my boot and placed the leg in a new kind of splint. It was a double plastic balloon, shaped like a boot, so that the limb rested on a cushion of air. To the inventor of that little item, my undying thanks. It saved me a heap of discomfort.

Periodically, the nurse reported to me on the latest newcomer to the clinic, saying that, if it were any comfort to me, each was worse off than I.

As plans were being made to fly me home to our orthopedist, I suddenly remembered something important I had left undone back on the slope. There were signs all over to warn me, too. I had forgotten to cover my Sitzmark!

Flying High

Arrangements had to be made to get me home. The doctor prescribed a plane. It would be quicker, more comfortable and relatively little more expensive than ground transportation.

The fact that it was an ambulance plane didn't lessen the importance I was beginning to feel. I

pretended that chartered air travel was old hat, and lay back to enjoy it. The doctor gave me a parting shot, and I was flying high before the plane left the ground.

I'm glad he did that 'cause if the truth were known I think flying is great—for someone else. It can be pleasurable, though, except for takeoff, in-flight, and landing. Whenever I fly, I usually help things along by pushing very hard into the floor to take off and land, and asking about the pilot's qualifications en route.

God, I really am scared. Not just because of flying, but this whole unreality. This isn't me, lying on the floor of this little plane bumping up and down with the air currents through the mountains. Someone's leg, not mine, is down there. It's un-whole, it feels ugly. I don't want it to be part of me.

Is that the way You feel about me, God? I'm an extension of You. You're perfect, and whole, and good. And when that inner part of me is imperfect, unwhole, and evil, wouldn't You like to be rid of me?

Despite all that, You love me. You accept me. You want me to be whole in my soul where it's much more important than in a leg. And You want it for my good, not Yours. It wouldn't make You any more God. But it would make me more complete.

I'm scared, God. I think that my great big man is scared, too. I can tell by his everything's-super-O K - all-right attitude. Give him strength through this turbulence in which we are flying, and that turbulence which is awaiting us below.

I wonder if David was a pilot. Otherwise, where did this flight record come from? "Your loving-

kindness extends to the heavens and Your faithfulness reaches to the skies."

Before the pilot felt the urge to warm up the engines, he wanted to see something tangible for his efforts. Hubby scrounged around, wired home, and borrowed to find the required two hundred dollars. With this impetus, the pilot was raring to go.

En route, my husband engaged him in conversation. How many trips did he make each week with this kind of broken down cargo? An average of ten to fifteen, the pilot explained. During "good" weeks when the slopes were icy, he profited from this Land-Slide business. When he had to fly to more distant places, he got paid three hundred dollars.

I was light-headed, but able to do some figuring. Ten trips at two or three hundred dollars apiece came to two or three thousand dollars. Deduct some for gas and maintenance. Not bad in the booming ski business.

He didn't even have to invest in comfortable cots for the cargo. I was lying on something that would have made a fold-up army cot feel like a waterbed. Right then and there I decided our next "togetherness" hobby would be flying lessons.

No Curtain Call

The medication began to wear off, but I was comfortable; in fact, quite chipper. I looked forward to my arrival at the airport. I could picture it. On the plane radio I soon would begin to hear the air traffic controller clearing the way for my emergency situation. Dozens of planes would have to circle the airfield, since we would have priority. Ambulances, patrol cars and policemen on motorcycles would keep the curious, shoving crowd at bay.

There would be flashing red lights and sirens. Reporters would take pictures and ask questions. Opera debuts were always exciting, but this debut would top them all. People would be lined up to get a glimpse of what was on the stretcher. In the dark, on the floor of the plane, I practiced smiling and waving to my fans—feebly, of course.

Things were looking up already. There would be no competition from other Basket Cases to detract from my Grand Entrance. A wild ride through the city streets with sirens screaming would keep attention high.

Foiled again! When we landed, not one policeman, motorcycle, flashing light, reporter, camera or circling airplane was in sight! Not even the on-the-ground ambulance ordered by the pilot was there. We waited in interminable, awful SILENCE.

The pilot, anxious to be rid of his heap of broken

bones so he could fly back for another set, finally radioed the tower. The tower spotted the ambulance miles away—at the other end of the field. It had gone to the wrong gate. When, eventually, I was settled into the ambulance, I felt cheated of all the drama that might have been.

To top it off, I could have gotten to the hospital faster by mule train, and the driver didn't see fit to use the siren one teensy little squeal.

But there was one small consolation. The handsome, young attendant who hovered over me showed sympathetic concern for my Condition. Perhaps I should have pretended more pain, or moaned now and then. When he observed how well I was getting along, he struck up a one-sided conversation. He asked all kinds of questions about religion, politics, and what he should get his girl for Christmas—then answered them himself.

When we arrived at the hospital, my bad luck was still holding! There wasn't a spectator on hand to appreciate my misfortune. I was carried quietly to my room without benefit of any sympathetic consolers to fuss over my sad plight. In opera, when I became "ill" or "died," there was always an audience to enjoy it.

Sometimes the cast enjoyed my "dying," too. During one performance when I was gasping my last twenty-minute breath, the hero came bursting onstage to embrace me once more. He evidently miscalculated his speed and the length of the stage, and he lunged at me so forcefully he sent me crashing to the floor.

It was the only time in the history of opera that rigor mortis set in, as I convulsed hysterically with laughter, and he emoted over the fate of his "dead" beloved.

Now in this real-life drama, everything was desperately dull. Maybe it was just as well. I was in no shape to take a curtain call.

The Boy Who Cried Wolf

It was time to notify the children. This was my Big Moment. Surely the *children* would properly appreciate my sorrowful plight. I reached for the telephone and prepared for the dramatic announcement. Thwarted again.

Just prior to my call, my teenage son, a big tease and practical joker, had answered another call. When he returned to the dinner table, he fabricated an amazingly prophetic story to his sisters, and the friends staying with them.

"That was the hospital," he invented. "Mother broke her leg." After his glee at their swallowing the story, the real call came, and he again answered the phone.

"Hi, Son."

"Hi, Mom. D'ja have a good time?"

"Well, yes—and no."

"Guess you're tired out. Glad you're back in town. There's just enough supper for you and Dad. Hurry home. Bye." *Bang* went the receiver.

I dialed again.

"Hello?"

"Jeff—this is Mother. I'm in the hospital with a broken leg."

Laughter. "Oh, sure, Mom. Wish you'd hurry home. I've got a date tonight, and it's my turn to clean up the kitchen."

Just then his father came back into my room.

Weakly I pleaded, "Daddy—they don't believe me. Do you think we should send them a wire?"

Father decisively reached for the phone.

"Son—Mom's . . ."

"Hi, Dad, where are ya? Glad ya had a good time. I really fooled the gang here. When the phone rang, I answered. It was my friend. I told everyone Mom broke her leg and was in the hospital!" The bombastic laughing hyena's voice came so loudly I could hear it even with my hands over my ears. "Then Mom called and tried to fool *me* and . . ."

"Jeff!" interrupted his dad. His voice was dark and

foreboding, the tone we all knew to be his I-am-about-to-issue-a-weighty-pronouncement voice. "We *are* at the hospital. Mom *did* break her leg—badly!"

This time it was his son's turn to be momentarily stunned.

"Really, Dad?" (Pause) "Nnnneeeeeeeeeeeeeeet-oh! Wait till I tell the kids at school! *It really happened!* Hey, Dad, I predicted it! Do you s'pose I am one of those 'sidekicks' who can tell what's gonna happen? Gosh, I better go off alone and predict what's gonna happen tomorrow!"

"Hold on, Son. You're no 'psychic'! You didn't predict *anything!* You just came up with another one of your practical jokes. You cried 'wolf' again. Now no one will believe you."

As his father predicted, no one believed Jeff when he tried to convince them I really had broken my leg. It was up to me to convince them with the Proof.

And, once again, the glamour and attention I was sure would be mine drained away before Aesop's real "wolf" came out of hiding.

Penurious Pioneer

Now there was a practical problem of major import to be solved. How would we get the ski pants off? Simple? Not for me. I had paid thirty dollars—on sale at that—for them, and wasn't about to see them cut to shreds. I might never go skiing again, but that made no difference. My thrifty rural upbringing did not permit anything to be thrown away. After an item of clothing had gone the last mile, it was made into something else and used some more.

Every time the nurses came toward me with their trusty scissors poised for action, I put up such a fuss they retreated. As surgery drew near, a decision had to be made.

Mustering all of my pioneer tenacity (the children's father calls it stubbornness), I pushed and tugged until the good leg was free. Laying the empty pant leg carefully beside the injured leg still in its plastic balloon, I commanded, "From here on, it's the doctor's problem. I don't care how he gets the pants off. But don't you *dare* let him cut them."

He didn't. He's a real genius. That was a neater trick than fixing up the engineering job on my leg. And, because of this thrifty quirk of mine, an interesting contribution was made to medical science. According to the orthopedist, there had been a minimum of swelling even with such extensive injury. In a remarkably short time the leg was ready to

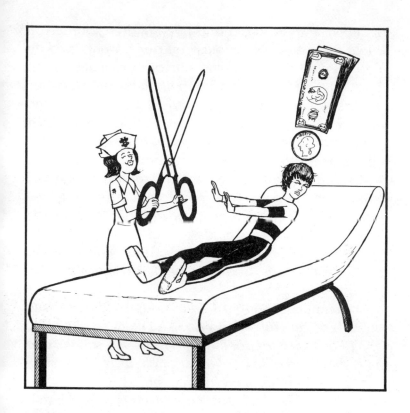

set. Keeping the stretch pants on had allowed normal circulation, and disallowed excessive swelling. My doctor was so enthusiastic about this discovery, he wrote various physicians in ski resorts about it.

He could have spared his secretary a lot of letter writing, though, by wiring them all the same short message, "Keep those pants on."

Dear Jesus, suddenly I find myself thinking of my childhood in the rolling plains of North Dakota. We really were penurious pioneers and poor—our family of seven: mama, papa and five children. But we all knew we were dearly loved by our parents and by You. I remember trudging out of our village to the meadows on the crunching melting snow to look for the first crocus. That lovely little flower represented the official harbinger of spring, and whoever found it was kind of special as everybody in school and at home celebrated the end of winter.

After the snows melted and the tall grasses grew, I would run out again into Your wonderful, vast, free meadows. I always found a special spot, and I would lie down completely hidden, and chew on a juicy green stem. I would look up into Your blue, blue sky and cotton clouds, and imagine all kinds of shapes in them.

Sometimes I thought I saw You, and I wondered about You and talked to You. You were so real. Why can't I believe like that little girl now—so simply, and with that kind of trust? Never again will I know such peace until I meet You in Heaven.

Isn't it too bad we put You into our little "boxes" when You are so great, so beautiful, so big, so loving and so wonderful?

Never-Never Land

There were the grey hours waiting for surgery. Medication kept me comfortable, but its pain-dulling effect could not still a nagging anxiety. If offended my sense of order to think of my tibia and fibula in such brash disarray.

I thought about David again. He had bone trouble, too. And he spoke about it a lot in his talks to God. He mentioned that his bones were disjointed, that when he was out of step with God, he felt it in his very bones. There were times when he must have been ill, unable to eat, and he lost a lot of weight. There were times when he could actually count his bones.

God, he was so like me—seesawing back and forth between super-faith, so-so faith, questioning-faith, and, many times, no-faith. He praises You one minute, then he gets uptight and scolds You soundly. He pats himself on the back when everything is right-on (he gives You some of the credit), and then fusses and stews about all the bad guys and problems of life that are about to do him in.

Now I'm on the down side of the seesaw again. I'm fearful of what's ahead. They're going to wheel me into that room with the bright lights and shadowy figures dressed up with funny clothes and masks as if they're going to a Halloween party.

Anything could happen in there, God. . . But

David never was entirely defeated. He knows You well enough as his Hope and Guide and Life and Maker to say, "When I fall it isn't fatal, for You hold me in Your hand. You're going to be absolutely delighted with each step I take."

Why do these comforting, beautiful thoughts come to me now during deep apprehension? Do they come from You? Who else would know, with such certainty, about the steps I will take again? Because YOU know, God, I'll come through with flying colors. I AM GOING TO WALK AGAIN!

As I was taken into the operating room, on what reminded me of our picnic table, everything was just too Quiet. There were no bright lights. No one rushed around with trays of surgical instruments waiting for the doctor to say, "Forceps, please."

I wondered where everyone was. Had they forgotten our seven o'clock appointment? After all my previous disappointments, I wanted this to be a Big Occasion. Maybe there would be a few small "undangerous" complications, so when friends would ask about My Operation, I wouldn't have to exaggerate too much.

As I was thinking about this, a green-clad form leaned over me. Things were getting exciting now—just like on television. Maybe he'd let me in on some of the hospital romances, scandal and gossip that you see on the soap operas.

But when he stuck a needle in my arm, I figured it was the anaesth — (that's as far as I can spell it). Before I could answer his "How are you?" I was out. This disturbed me later, since I don't like to be rude. Had I been able, I would have had a good deal to tell him about the State of my Health.

The Cast: Marvelous Monstrosity

I groped my way back to consciousness.

"God, You and I have come through one of our deepest valleys."

The time for the Unveiling was at hand. Since this was my first cast, I wanted it to measure up to what I had imagined. I was not to be disappointed. Expectantly I lifted the blanket to view for the first time the accessory which was going to be part of me for a long time to come.

The shock was unnerving! My doctor had wrought a modern work of art. This piece of unearthly sartorial splendor would not only be the envy of Orthopedics, it would put the Martians to shame. The cast was massive. It engulfed my right side from big toe to thigh. As if that were not dramatic enough, this ingenious man had sculpted out of plaster the "piece de resistance." Four knobs, the size of Ping-Pong balls protruded from each side. They held steel traction pins in place. I knew then why the male nurse had wheeled me up to surgery on a picnic table. I was trussed up like a chicken on a rotisserie.

As time passed, I became quite attached to those knobs. They were useful as handles to lift the leg. As a place for the kids to doodle. As a back scratcher for the dog.

Best of all, the Knobs were a wonderful conversation piece. When friends came to call, and conversation lagged, I would lift my leg via the "handles" in a well-planned gesture. This brought on another round of talk, the length of which depended on how much I chose to embellish the story.

A few weeks later, the Cast was enhanced some more. At first the knee was completely enclosed and therefore immovable. Trying to sit took some doing. I had to balance precariously on that small part of my posterior not covered with plaster, while the rest of me practiced levitation. In order to lean against the back of a chair, I did so at a forty-five degree angle with only my shoulders touching.

Whenever my orthopedist was around, I tried to

look as uncomfortable as possible. This didn't require much play-acting and apparently my performance was convincing, because it brought results. Again our good doctor outdid himself. He designed a device so grotesque as to make the original cast look like a Rodin masterpiece. For this, he sent me to a rehabilitation expert.

The cast was cut off just below the knee. My famous knobs were carved off, exposing the pins. To these were fastened two stainless steel bars running from heel to thigh where a leather girdle was attached. This could be unstrapped for washing, but, much more important—for scratching. To keep the bars in place, yards of plaster bandage dipped in resin were wrapped round and round over the pins. The End Result reminded me of a mummy with the mumps.

At the knee was a hinge which, when unlocked, enabled me to bend my leg. When locked, it provided stability for standing and walking. This was another contribution to medicine, since, to the doctor's knowledge, it was the first time such a scheme had been tried.

Before this aesthetic atrocity was added, people usually gave the knob getup a good look and went on about their business. Now, they invariably did a double take and made a note to get their eyes checked. It was so ugly the doctor made me promise never to tell anyone who did this to me.

But I didn't care. I had my Knee back. And I could sit like everyone else. Levitation just wasn't my thing!

Hospital Fetishes

Hospitals are good places to be when you are sick. But don't expect to get any rest there. I think there is a Master Plan in hospitals directing all personnel to wake up any patient who accidentally falls asleep, day or night.

It could be that they take very seriously the command to wake—the coming of the Lord is nearer than expected—and they want to be sure everyone is ready.

Usually the procedure is something like this: A nurse gives you a sleeping pill or shot. Just after you go from Morphine to Morpheus, someone comes in, shines a flashlight in your face and asks if you are sleeping. You try it again, fall asleep and someone drops a bedpan. It continues to roll down the hall with a terrible clang!

Once more now. Just dozing off and the maintenance crew comes in to fix a leaky faucet, or holler, "Go back to sleep. Wrong room!"

One night during my first good sleep in my one hundred twenty-five dollar a day room (that's why I had trouble getting to sleep), two men came in, noisily talking, turned on the light, banged doors and clanged heavy hardware. They were rigging up a set of pull-up bars over my bed—AT THREE O'CLOCK IN THE MORNING!

Needless to say, there was no more sleep that

night, and I used the time to good advantage plotting ways of getting even. I thought about filling my bedpan from the faucet, putting it up over the door and sending out a call for them. But as it would for a long time to come, Ye Olde Caste prevented me from implementing this Ingenious Plan!

The best way to get even, I decided, was not to use those darn bars. That would show 'em!

There ought to be some courses offered on what to expect in hospitals, including Temperature Taking and Bedpans. After all the experience I've had, I still don't know where that mysterious under-the-tongue

Thermometer Holder is.

Taking your Temperature is a hospital fetish. I don't know how often this is done in twenty-four hours, but I think it is twenty-four times.

I'm sure this is necessary, but along with Taking your Temperature, the nurses ought to take your Blood Pressure, too. About the fourteenth time they jab that thermometer under the tongue, you worry about clamping down too hard, biting off the end of it, and dying of mercury poisoning. Before the nurse gets back to get her silly old thermometer, your Blood Pressure could get awfully high—or just plain quit.

Other fearful things can happen, too. One day Henry, a young aide who kept things lively for everyone, passed by my door to say hello, carrying a whole basketful of thermometers. I asked him if he was going around again poking all those things into patients' mouths.

"Not *these*," he grinned, as he sauntered down the hall.

Hospital Specialists

One reason you don't get any rest in hospitals is the highly specialized time in which we live. Doctors are a good example of this. There are many kinds of specialists in a particular field of Specialization. There is the bone specialist, the hand-bone specialist, the right-hand-bone specialist, and the thumb of-the-right-hand-bone specialist.

I knew that about doctors, but I wasn't prepared for the hospital with all its specialists. There is not just one specialist who comes in to clean your room, and then leaves so you can get some sleep. It's more like a twenty-four hour police lineup. You used to be able to tell them apart. A nurse wore a white uniform, and a doctor wore a white smock over his trousers. But now—blue coats, with blue pants; blue coats with white pants; all white coats and pants, male and female; white uniforms with a hat; white uniforms without a hat, and on and on.

The lineup starts. First to come is the fresh-linen specialist, followed by the bedmaking specialist. After that, the floor-mop specialist, followed by the sink-cleaning specialist, the mirror-wiping specialist, and the toilet-bowl specialist.

In addition, there is the plant-watering specialist. But this specialist only waters plants, not cut flowers, and my beautiful bouquets began to droop. There was only one thing to do. One evening when Hubby came to see me, I dubbed him Grand Marshal

Watering Specialist of the Order of Cut Flowers. Secretly, of course, so he wouldn't get in trouble with the Flower Waterer's Union.

Some of my favorite specialists are the women who work many hours at hospitals without pay. They have names like Grey, Pink and Auxilian, and they specialize in everything.

A few of their specialties include: Rocking sick children; walking miles in hospital corridors and up and down stairs to get supplies needed immediately; filling out menus for those whose eyes are bad or who can't read; carrying authorized lab and X-ray forms to the proper places; pushing a "goodie" cart for patients well enough to shop; wheeling happy patients to their cars on going-home day; pausing to give a caring word or cheer and encouragement to sad, lonely, sick, sometimes frightened people. In short, God's creatures in a time of distress.

Their most important specialty is the giving of self, with a fierce loyalty and devotion. They believe with a passion in what they are doing, and that without their help hospitals could not carry on. Do you want to know something? I think they're right!

Another important specialist is the IWGA—the Ice Water Girl Aide. I had never taken a drink of ice water at 5:30 in the morning in my whole life. But the IWGA wanted to be sure that, if I were to begin that habit, there would be fresh ice water to drink.

At 5:30 in the afternoon when, at the end of a long and restless day I craved and desired fresh ice water, it was impossible to get. So I gave up that idea while in the hospital, and developed an insatiable thirst for ice water at 5:30 in the morning. It persists to this day.

This then wakens my husband, and leads to all kinds of problems or possibilities.

Special Specialist

I'm lucky, God, to have so many specialists attending to my needs. Some of them are happy, and they give me happiness when I get low. Some are sad, I can tell. They have lots of problems. We talk, and when I tell them they can give them all to You, they are not so sad for awhile. Remember, God, the beautiful black lady who comes in the middle of every long night? She knows I can't sleep and we talk—about our families, our hopes, and how we feel about You and Your Son. Now, what if I hadn't been in the accident? I wouldn't be in this place, and I would have missed her love and friendship.

And my doctor-specialist, Jim Friend. We didn't know each other very well before this. We had, however, gone through a lot together some years ago when Julie was small. Remember when she was a tiny baby, toddling around, and my old car backed down the hill, knocked her down and pinned her there? How her little head and arms served as a wedge that stopped the car? I can see her under the wheel, white and so quiet. I thought she was dead. Do You remember how, through a miracle, my friend knew how to get the car off of her because of a special driving lesson her mother had taught her years before?

Your special specialist, Dr. Friend, was the only orthopedist available and he came to the hospital to take care of her. How come You sent him?

"How will you take care of her broken bones?" we asked in anxious fear.

We'll never forget his answer, "With these two hands," and he lifted them in a gesture fraught with compassion, determination and strength. Those beautiful skillful hands did their work and our baby was fully restored to us.

Dear God, when I think of the work of Your hands, and how You used his hands, I can answer David's question, "What is man, that Thou dost take thought of him?" You thought of Julie, and You gave her back to us—whole. You do care. How very much You care!

Thank You for Dr. Friend. He didn't know You then—the way he does now. And neither did I. I could feel the pain inside of him then; and again now, even with all his cheerful bluffing, when he came to see me after studying the X-rays. We both knew again there could be bad problems. But he ministers to the spirit as well as the body when broken, scared people come to him. He always gives You the credit, "I set the bones, but another Physician heals them."

Dear God, YOU are the Super-Specialist. Unlike all the other kinds of specialists, YOU all by Yourself can take care of all our needs. At home or at work when something goes wrong, we pick up the phone and call the electrician, the carpenter, the plumber, the doctor or a tax specialist. Inside of us when something goes wrong, we pick up the phone and call a friend, a counselor, the druggist or a minister, and we expect instant answers. We don't call YOU!

Please God, help me make better use of my Heavenly phone. It's the only line that never gives me the busy signal.

A Little Child Shall Lead Them

There were serious moments and valleys—many times. Recurring waves of occasional depression, even dread, as the prospect of prolonged "incasteration" rolled over me. To cope with them I was forced to reassess values and reexamine my all too immature faith.

As I took inventory, these were the facts: I had a bad injury. There would be a long period of recuperation. Several alternatives lay before me. I could put myself on a shelf and self-pityingly withdraw. After all, what good could come out of a shattered limb? What beauty was there in this ugliness? Or, I could embark on a New Adventure. This latter idea I fought like a tiger. It would demand discipline and effort. How much easier to give in.

Somewhere I had read that no prayer is complete unless half the time is spent in listening. As was my habit, *I* preferred to do all the talking. It was difficult, but upon one occasion, lying on that bed, I forced myself to listen. Out of a maze of thoughts, one idea gained the upper hand. What had happened was far less important than the attitude I took toward it.

At last, I could really put to the test the "theory" that I could find inner contentment without necessarily being satisfied. And I *could* do *everything* through Christ, because I would rely on His strength. These words of Paul were no longer a platitude to me.

By an act of the will I could and would apply this thought, though I would not always be successful.

A cherished incident several years ago pointed up graphically how "good" could come out of "bad."

When Julie, our blond, blue-eyed "caboose" was five, we had our first opportunity to visit the Bad Lands of South Dakota. Upon arriving there, parking the car and looking around, we were disappointed that there was nothing unusual to see, except more flat plains. But as we followed the guideposts, suddenly we came upon it. A panorama of grotesque

formations, eroded canyons and layered striations which stretched before us into infinity. The sun was setting, and as it cast long shadows on this desolate, wasted wilderness, it painted magnificent colors on the landscape. The view was breathtaking, and in the deathly silence we were speechless.

Overwhelmed by the strange beauty all around her, Julie, who had tripped on ahead, stopped abruptly at the edge of a jagged plateau. In childish delight at the sight of these *Bad* Lands, she clapped her hands and shouted, "My, what a wonderful place for *God* to live!"

The parallel, I realize now, was striking. If I were willing, my Wilderness of Despair could be a "wonderful place for God to live."

Months later, this little child was to lead me once again. It was during a particularly trying attempt to maneuver in the kitchen. Feeling clumsy and inept, in frustration I threw a spatula on the floor and wept angrily. As she came upon the scene, Julie shook her head, put out her hands in a "how could you be so forgetful?" gesture, and chided, "But, Mom, remember? You've got GOD going for you!"

Crutches—Bless 'Em!

It was time for a new phase of Cast Life—crutches. I was wheeled to the therapist's bailiwick, a tiny room stuffed with all sorts of railings and contraptions, for my first lesson. With great care I was taught to cling to the railings, step on my good leg, and swing through with the cast. This worked out rather well. I was sure I would master the technique readily.

The therapist adjusted a pair of crutches, showed me where to place them against my side a few inches below the armpits, and turned me loose. Then, I was on my own.

With fear and trepidation I began the step—the Swing Through. Success! Back and forth down the corridor a few times and I was onto it. Evidently this first major exertion since I had forsaken my skiing career was too much, and I began to feel faint. I had often practiced fainting onstage, but here was the real thing, superbly done, and authentic.

The therapist was right behind me. He caught me under the arms and, squatting down, allowed me to rest on his knee. As I settled in to enjoy and make the most of this opportunity, he lowered, and lowered, and lowered me, until I was lying flat on the corridor floor.

A passing X-ray technician took a disdainful look, stepped over me, and walked on, grumbling something about people fainting in front of his door.

After all, *his* department had a reputation to maintain.

As I became proficient in using crutches, it became obvious that the biggest annoyance was their predisposition to falling down. If I put them on the floor, they were in somebody's way. If I propped them against the wall, they came clattering down like the walls of Jericho. They must have fallen a million times.

If I were an inventor, I would invent a stand for crutches. It would probably improve the mental health of the country considerably. Nerves are easily frayed by the repeated clatter of falling crutches.

During my ten months with these Abominable Stilts, my son and older daughter, both of whom are taller than I, joined the Crutch Club. Each fractured foot bones slightly in Physical Education classes. Fortunately, they did not have to wear casts, but had to keep weight off the fractured area for a few days.

It was bad enough with three members of the same household causing Crutch Jams. But when these kingsized, obstreperous adolescents substituted their crutches for mine, it was downright annoying. Hiding behind the door, they guffawed at my attempts to fit their oversized crutches under my arm.

The other day my dearly beloved phoned, saying he had a story to tell me.

"It's funny as a crutch," he enthused.

"*That's* not funny!" I retorted.

Concert in the Corridor

After a week in the hospital I began to feel like a person again. It was the Christmas season, and even my septic-white temporary home took on a festive look. Nurses put up decorations. Carolers came to sing. Cards and gifts poured in to the patients.

Despite all this, Hospital Blues set in. Hospital Blues happen after the initial excitement and shock wear off. You begin to take inventory and wonder what kind of idiot would get into such a situation. In my case, there was further cause.

It was the season of love and good will. Other mothers were busy baking, shopping, and hiding Santa's secrets. This one wasn't.

Patiently, my Instructor led me to see that for this very reason I could, if I were open to His Spirit, experience my most significant Christmas. Circumstances spared me from being bombarded by empty incantations of "Deck the Halls," "Noel" and "Rudolph" to promote the sale of stuff for stockings. I could center down on the true Wonder of what Christmas is all about.

Crutching down the corridor one afternoon for a bit of exercise, I chanced to hear the cry of a new baby coming from the clean, warm nursery. My mind turned to thoughts of another Baby born in a cold, smelly cave, and bedded down in a feeding trough. Even as His mother cradled Him in her arms, so too,

He cradled a Destiny within Himself. And two thousand years later in a hospital room, He came to me offering, again, everything He wanted the whole world to receive the *first* time He came. Peace, joy, forgiveness, love, and healing of soul and body. He came to give Life, the most important gift of all, and so few will take it. What an array of gifts. And best of all, I didn't have to battle the crowds to shop for them.

One afternoon a friend came to visit. "Look," she suggested, "you have a broken leg, but what about your voice? Quit moping about shopping, and give the gift you carry around with you all the time. Let's

give our music and bring Christmas into the hospital."

Thus it was that we planned and presented a concert in the corridor. I sang from a wheelchair. She accompanied on her violin. It was perhaps one of the most appreciated concerts either of us had presented anywhere. There were thank-you's and applause by both patients and staff. One gentleman patient clapped louder and longer than the rest. He even shouted a gusty "Bravo!"

"Now there," I thought, "is a man who really knows talent when he hears it."

The Clapping Gentleman

I wanted to meet this person with such excellent taste in music. Within a few hours via the hospital Underground, messages were flying back and forth between the Clapping Gentleman and the Debilitated Diva. He also was a singer. When stricken, he was appearing in our city. Since he was recuperating nicely from his illness, he was free to be up and around.

Again, with the help of the Underground, we arranged a rendezvous in my room. I hummed happily as I tried to salvage a hairdo and see if I could remember how to apply some makeup. At the appointed time he arrived, and it was not long before we were chatting like old friends. We discussed our common interest, the operatic roles we knew, and the places we had sung.

Quite spontaneously we began singing one of the lovely Victor Herbert duets. So enthralled were we with our harmony, we made no effort at pianissimo. Indeed, it became fortissimo. Halfway through our extemporaneous concert, an executive-type matron (who evidently had *no* musical taste) padded down the hall in typical hospitalian efficiency, and barged into the room.

"Sshh!" she admonished, "you're waking the other patients," and gave the door a more-than-needed-to-close-it shove. (I thought we were saving the staff a lot

of time going around shining flashlights in everybody's face.)

We continued through this hardly noticed inter-
ruption, not missing a note. We started a second
chorus, probably with more gusto now that the door
was closed.

I don't know if it was Temperature Taking time, or
if the matron had had enough. At any rate, before we
could finish the duet, our matron-shusher marched in
brusquely. When our mouths were opened wide for a

high note, she popped a thermometer in each! Sure hope she didn't get them out of *Henry's* basket.

That evening when the doctor came to see me, I asked him if I could go home. Also, I related the events of the afternoon and the nurse's ingenius way of stopping our singing. I felt he should get *my* version before he got *hers*.

"Let me out tomorrow, Doctor," I begged, "or I'll sing my favorite aria from *"Traviata,"* and it has four high 'C's!'"

God, where do you suppose the Clapping Gentleman is now? Charming and gifted—yet I sensed a loneliness and longing in him. You remember, when we talked often during those hospital days, he told me he knew about You and Your Son. But he didn't feel a need to know You.

For a few days he became very ill again, and my sweet husband and I went to see him often. We asked if he minded listening in while we asked You to care for him and show him Your love. And it brought tears to his eyes. God, reach out to him wherever he is right now.

As in the old spiritual, Clapping Gentleman, "Did you ever come to know my Jesus"? Because when you do, you'll never stop clapping.

Languishing

Perhaps the doctor was concerned about more extemporaneous concerts. Or maybe he considered the trouble he might have getting future patients admitted if word got out that they sang. Probably it was a matter of my being ready to leave. At any rate, I was out the next day.

My Better Half arrived to take home his lopsided wife and a carload of accumulated accoutrements. The children had cleaned the house, decorated the Christmas tree, and had a welcome fire awaiting me—this time in the fireplace. They must have remembered my wrath from earlier years when they preferred fires in closets. It was good to be home, with all of them fussing over me.

Friends came by to further brighten my homecoming. They invited all of us out to a celebration dinner. Though it sounded wonderful after the lonely hospital trays, I was a bit hesitant. It might not be proper to socialize the day I came home from the hospital. Furthermore, I had better not appear too well too soon if I wanted to make the most of my recuperative days ahead.

Way down deep was a secret desire to do some languishing. I recalled reading about Elizabeth Barrett Browning who languished delicately, while Robert wrote beautiful love poetry to her. I had seen Mimi and Violetta, opera characters, languishing on a chaise, singing with a lot of vigor for girls as sick as they were supposed to be. I confess that the glamour of it lured me like the Pipes of Pan. I had no way of knowing how I would tire of languishing in the months to come.

Will there ever be an end to this prison, God? I'm so weary from the heaviness of this cast. I'm becoming turned in to myself, not tuned in to You. I'm pushing out my husband, my family and my dearest friends. Loving and concerned as they are about me, they make me resentful. They are up and around and "normal," functioning as I used to do. But I feel ugly, unfeminine, and I'm a drag on everybody.

I, who love life, have loads of vitality, and so many things to do. I, who should be doing for my family and for others who need my help. I, who once thought I was indispensable to my home, husband, children and church. And to my students and relatives and friends!

It seems as if now my illness is not broken bones. It's my spirit. I feel defeated—useless, and literally, down-cast. I can diagnose my own problem because it's "I" trouble. The kind an opthalmologist cannot treat. Is that what You want me to see, God? That I think I can do it all by myself, without You? And, if I keep on in my own ego trip, I don't need You? To be honest, God, life goes on pretty much as usual whether or not I wear this cast. That's tough to take!

Cast! Cast! Cast! It appears hundreds of times in Your Book. Cast down, cast out, cast lots, cast out demons. It usually means to get rid of something. How I long to get rid of this cast, God, but I think You want me to get rid of far more debilitating encumbrances.

David, too, had these battles. But one day, after one of his fiercest personal struggles, he turned it all around, acknowledged his "I" trouble, and rooted it out with the best tranquilizer offered to the ill, the troubled, and the disturbed.

"CAST YOUR BURDEN UPON THE LORD AND HE WILL SUSTAIN YOU."

David does not infer instant panacea for all of life's troubles, but he knows that never again will he have to bear them alone.

God, isn't it great? I don't have to carry this awful cast and my "I" trouble alone. I CAST it on You.

That first afternoon home from the hospital brought a telephone call which ended languishing for that day. It was a woman who had always reminded me of gloomy Eeyore in *Winnie the Pooh*. I don't know what she does. I think she's a Professional Mourner.

"I just heard about your accident and wanted to cheer you up," she said in a doleful tone. "Six years ago my uncle fell and broke his hip. He lay in excruciating pain, just out of reach of the phone for four hours . . ." continued the sepulchral voice.

"He's dead now. Died several years ago. I just know it was from complications which developed during those four hours he lay there trying to get help."

As she went on to describe in graphic and

depressing detail that, and another friend's recent surgery, my mind went into action. I added up the hours I was on the mountainside and in emergency centers waiting for medical treatment. It came to exactly *four*! My days were numbered!

When my Ambassador of Good Tidings concluded, I slammed the receiver down and announced to my startled guests, "I accept your invitation to dinner! Saint Peter will just have to audition a few more sopranos before he gets this one to join his choir!"

Up the Staircase?

We live in a roomy, old two-story house, and I was eager to get back to it. The evening before I was released from the hospital, my doctor came in to give me some last minute instructions. In addition, he raised a crucial question which had not occurred to me.

"How are you going to get up those stairs to your bedroom?"

The cast was set at an angle which made it dangerous to hop up on one leg. A second way was rejected because having two big men around to carry me up and down seemed a bit impractical. The doctor suggested that for the duration I stay on the ground floor.

After he left, I got a real case of the Blues thinking about my wonderful Bed Warmer, and how I'd miss snuggling up to all six-foot-two of him. I visualized every possible way of getting up to my own bed, but each time ran into an insurmountable barrier. The more I thought about it, the more obsessed I became with finding a way up That Staircase. My Light Bulb came on as the nurse handed me a pill.

I would go up that staircase—BACKWARDS! I would sit on the first step and back myself up one riser at a time holding the crutches with one hand. Coming down I could reverse the procedure. Later on, I would use the bannister for support and climb in standing position. Pleased with my Plan I relaxed and slept like a baby.

After eleven months of implanting this habit into the mind, it has been difficult to break. Even now, whenever I come to stairs, people stop and stare curiously as I pause, turn around, and begin up the staircase BACKWARDS.

Hey, God, it's beginning to work. This business of "casting" my problems on You—something as insignificant as going upstairs. No one can tell me that You didn't plant that idea about how to get up the stairs.

You do care—about every little thing. You who made the universe full of space capsules much more dependable than anything NASA has to offer.

And You care about me—vacillating, disobedient, complaining, selfish, and all the rest. But You know I want to be something much better. And You're showing me that Bad Lands can be turned into Good Lands.

God, You so love the world—and me, too.

Can You Top This?

Once I began going places there were a variety of responses and reactions to my cast. People were interested, concerned, sympathetic. In retrospect, I came to some fascinating conclusions.

Most individuals who had endured a similar experience, either their own or that of someone else, wanted to share it. If they related a first person happening, the details were generally moderate and the outcome optimistic. If they spoke of someone else, the description often became grim and gory. The outcome was pessimistic, even drastic. Often the closing remark was, "He's had nothing but trouble ever since!"

The list of harrowing tales was endless. The clerk in a shoe store where I tried to buy *one* shoe, the waitress in the restaurant, the painter who came to paint for us, a service appliance man—all had grim stories to tell.

A woman I didn't know stopped by my table in a coffee shop and, in Thespian style complete with gestures, reenacted the scene of the day *her* cast came off. Observing that her foray into the field of the dramatic arts had made its intended impression, she walked "off stage" theatrically with nary a limp.

One of the extreme illustrations of Bad News was the thoughtless babbling of another woman in a beauty shop. It was just a few weeks after my initiation as a Castaway, so I was vulnerable. She told of a young girl's accident resulting in a serious break. As she rattled on, spelling out the complications, I sensed Impending Doom and begged her not to go further. However, nothing could halt Calamity Jane who, caught up in her oratory, moved on to the climax. Over my protestations, she topped anything I was to hear in those many months. Victoriously she announced Things became so bad, the leg had to be amputated.

I was shaking when I left the beauty shop. Had I come out looking as glamourous as Zsa Zsa, evoking

whistles and catcalls from a shipload of sailors on leave, I wouldn't have heard them.

I'm slipping into another valley. What if that terrible thing should happen to me? What if my leg doesn't heal? What if I have complications?

What if—what if—what if?

What if I would let You keep all the what-ifs I cast upon You?

Jesus said to a whole lot of What-if-ers: "Worrying about what-ifs tomorrow won't add one thing to your living this day. You already have enough to think about. Chances are that most of these what-ifs won't happen. And, if they do, your Heavenly Father will take care of them."

God, What-If I would do that? Isn't that the only What-If You'll accept?

And Then There Were These

Memories. Of friends. Friends who waited during surgery. Friends who stood by as I hovered between darkness and light. Friends who prayed with waiting family. Who fed and cleaned for the family. Who phoned, visited, who bolstered my sagging spirits, and reassured us. Friends who sent loving letters, gifts, flowers, silly little things to make me laugh—all expressions of a deepening love we were experiencing together. The kind of friends who didn't just say if-you-need-anything-let-me-know; they just *did*.

Jesus, for the first time I am the recipient of this kind of love because of illness. I am beginning to understand the essence of Your oft-quoted words, "I was sick and you visited Me. Anything you did for anyone, however insignificant—or so you thought—you did it for Me."

These beautiful people carried me on through to Your healing Presence as surely as did the friends of the man who was lowered down through the roof to encounter You. You told him, and You tell me through these—"Take up your bed, and WALK." I don't believe You meant just physically. You want all of us to walk victoriously in our hearts and minds and souls and strength because we walk with You.

There were many people who were not prophets

of doom like the lady in the beauty shop. They possessed the gift of empathy and went out of their way to lift my sagging spirit as the months wore on.

Our Julie had for several years enjoyed an imaginary playmate she named Lonta. Often Lonta left for long periods of time, as Julie got older, to reappear again unexpectedly. One day when I was in the doldrums, Julie informed me Lonta was back. "But she has a broken leg like you and in a cast bigger than yours."

"Poor Lonta," I commiserated. "How is she doing?"

"Better than you, Mother. She's healing a lot faster," came the answer in a tone of slight reprimand.

Another time during one of my will-it-never-end spells, and floods of tears, she took me in her arms on my bed, and, in a rocking motion, patted me. She—the adult; I—the child.

My best friend, my husband, often took me for rides in the country and let me talk, be silent, cry, scold, or limp around on my crutches to help me free my spirit, though my body was imprisoned.

One woman stands out in my memory. As I was struggling to open a door into a supermarket, she held it for me, then said knowingly, "I understand, my dear. I was in a cast, too."

She echoed the wise words of an ancient writer, which says that anxious hearts are very heavy, but a word of encouragement does wonders.

Her ten words were better than any medical prescription. God bless you, Unknown Lady, wherever you are.

Traumatic Triumvirate

I looked forward to going to church again. I wanted to be with my many friends, hear the music and listen to my minister's messages. My return that first Sunday morning turned out to be a grand reunion. I didn't mind at all answering the oft-repeated question, "How are you?" I was glad to hear everyone say, "You look great!"

But, as the weeks and months wore on and they asked "How is the leg doing?" I couldn't give any flip answers because things *were* a bit slow. In fact, I got downright annoyed when a friend who broke a hip and didn't have to wear a cast reported on her amazing progress, and I couldn't. I did not discover until I was out of the cast that new bone growth had shown up on the X-rays where no cast was involved at a much earlier date. Therefore, despite my "I'm doing great" replies I wasn't sure.

And the weeks and months in church that followed proved to be somewhat disconcerting, too. I guess I took it too personally, but why did they insist on singing hymns like, "Lord, Plant My Feet on Higher Ground," "Walking in the Steps of the Savior," and "Stand Up, Stand Up for Jesus"—all four verses, and we *never* sing that hymn sitting down!

Even the choir sang anthems about my condition: "Why Am I *Cast* Down, O Lord," and "He Will not Let Your Foot Be Moved"!

But, my beloved minister beat everything when he preached on texts and subjects about "Man's Fallen State," "Climb up to a Higher Place," and "A Broken Vessel." Those were bad enough, but when he preached on "Ezekiel's Dry Bones," that did it! I am sure he looked straight at me through the entire sermon.

When I thought about his visits with me in the hospital, I had to forgive him. He brought me much cheer and inspiration and helped me to believe that God had in mind for me complete recovery and restoration.

Several other pastors in the community stopped often to say "hi" when they went by my room on their way to visiting folks. Once these ministers did shake me up a bit. On that occasion, *three* clergymen were at my bedside at the same time. This left me quite uptight as I later pondered the significance of their simultaneous visitations. I couldn't be sure if I were headed for Heaven a good deal sooner than I had anticipated, or whether it would take that many preachers to snatch me away from the gaping jaws of the Other Place!

For several days I reflected upon their visit. I was reminded of one of my favorite "preacher" jokes.

A little boy returned home from school one day, and crossing the patio in his back yard, he spotted a lizard. He chased it, and finally cornered it on all fours. He grabbed the tail and looked for a rock. When he found one, he hit the lizard over the head a few times until it became quite listless. He looked at it for awhile, then decided to scare his mom.

He picked it up again by the tail and ran across the

patio, up the steps and through the back door. He was unaware that the preacher had come to call. Bursting into the house, he ran through the kitchen and into the living room, shouting excitedly, "Mom, Mom, guess what! I was crossing the patio after school and I saw this lizard. I trapped it in a corner, found a big rock and hit it over the head a few times. . ." He spotted the minister talking with his mother. Instantly he exchanged his gleeful smile for a woeful frown, and concluded soberly, "Then the Lord took him home."

As I reflected upon the visit of the TRAUMATIC TRIUMVIRATE, I hoped that the Lord had something else in store than taking me Home just yet!

College Daze

My unexpected drop-out from society caused complications in another area of my life. I was commuting one hundred miles each way one day a week for some graduate work at a university. Four weeks remained until the semester break. To quit now was out of the question.

But the thought of returning to school in my bizarre costume, to say nothing of my red-faced embarrassment over what had happened the *only* day of the semester I had cut, made me feel and look like the Reluctant Dragon.

Maybe one way to stem the tide would be to get to each class as early as possible, and to try to sit in the back of the room. It was difficult to achieve anonymity, though, with the contraption I was sporting. Having drawn the attention I'd been looking for, I now didn't want it.

There were some put-your-best-foot-forwards, and shake-a-legs from fellow students. Professors looked condescendingly at this mother-turned-student distracting sprouting intellectuals from digesting their Pearls of Wisdom.

One class I dreaded more than the rest. The presiding professor had done his best to discourage me from enrolling in school and commuting "so far." He suggested I take up knitting instead. This made me all the more determined to earn an "A" in his class.

He was a slight man, not tall, Prussian, proper, and he rarely smiled except at his own spurious attempts at humor. When he did smile, I had the feeling his face would crack and his moustache split down the middle. And he scared me to death.

On my first day back, A.C. (After Cast), I wanted especially to avoid him. But I did not know the class had been moved from the top story of one building across campus to the second story of another. Now I was in trouble. I needed help with my books and music manuscripts. My husband, who had helped me to the original classroom, was gone.

Class had begun across campus, and with each passing minute I dreaded confrontation with That Professor. I was alone. Not another soul was in the building this hour of the night. I wondered if it were this quiet on the moon.

After what seemed like an eternity, the glorious sound of footsteps landed on my waiting ears. As quickly as I could, I crutched my way to the door. Finally, the Owner of the Footsteps came into view, and he got his first glimpse of this refugee from a disaster area. He blinked his eyes, caught his breath, and then graciously answered my SOS.

He carried the books as I worked my way down one flight of stairs, across campus, and up another staircase, *backwards, of course.* I thanked him and he left me at the door to await my fate.

What a sight I must have been! Half of me in plaster, leaning unsteadily on the crutches, hanging onto a satchel of heavy books, waiting for the Last

Judgment pronouncement from That Professor.

All eyes were on me during an interminable silence. He studied me for a long moment, shook his head unbelievingly, then broke into a broad grin, "Happy New Year! *However* you are, welcome back!"

In the ensuing weeks, That Professor and I gained a new and mutual respect for each other. At the end of the term, I carried home—along with all the other paraphernalia—my badge of achievement: A proudly earned "A."

Generation Gape

During the previous months at school B.C. (Before Cast), I tried to acquaint myself with more than my major field of study. I wanted to get to know the students and their thinking. I listened with keen interest to their soap-boxing in the student square. There was plenty of opportunity to do some wool-gathering in the cafeteria.

But I was Over Thirty. For the most part I got the ten-foot-pole treatment.

However, one day A.C., as I was making my way backwards up some steps leading across an open court to the library, I was Noticed! One young, bearded, bedraggled, bedangled, barefoot fellow, observing my cautious attempt at movement with attached accoutrements, bestirred himself.

He Gaped at me for a long moment, no doubt wondering if he were still on a "trip." He shook his head convulsively and blinked. Then convinced no "trip" could be this bad, he acted. Leisurely he gathered himself up from the lawn where he had been "meditating" and asked if he could be of assistance.

I was flattered. *I had arrived!* I had bridged the Generation Gap. Perhaps this Flower Child turned Boy Scout figured the Establishment could use a little help since it was in enough trouble already.

Sometime later, I saw this same pitiful heap of humanity so high on drugs that *he* could not help *me*. Instead I talked with him about a kind of experience that would require only one "fix," and bring him real and eternal Reality. A Guide, a Counselor, an Instructor, a Saviour—wiser than any college professor on this or any other campus.

As I continued to tell him about Jesus, how Jesus had come to give him life, this lonely searching empty young man gradually came down from his drug-induced high. And he was lifted higher than he ever imagined possible, by One who went past his bloodstream—directly into his heart.

Getting in and out of the college library was quite a feat. Everyone entering and leaving was carefully searched for books and materials that were improperly "borrowed." It was difficult for me to go through the narrow turnstile at any time. With my additional encumbrances I could have used some help from a tightrope artist. The opening simply wasn't wide enough for crutches, books and me.

After much experimentation, I found the best way to get through was sideways. The timing had to be exact as I shoved the bar and leaped a huge step, with the ever-present possibility of horrible consequences.

While I balanced, shoved and leaped, much like a racehorse at the starting gate, some enterprising students stood off to the side betting on the odds.

"Think she'll make it?"

"I doubt it."

"She just might do it."

"What are the chances?"

"Hundred to one."

"Bet you a buck she doesn't."

"Lay ya ten to one she does."

It was good the semester ended when it did, or I might have been picked up for contributing to the delinquency of betting minors.

Cleaning and Scratching

Keeping clean with twenty extra pounds of baggage was pretty discouraging. Every time I watched a deodorant commercial on television I had the feeling "my best friends wouldn't tell me."

For the first nine months, the old fashioned sponge bath worked out well, except for those who cleaned up after me. When I sponge, it's like taking a shower without the stall. Water everywhere. Somehow this makes me feel cleaner.

When the pins were removed and the time came for a shorter cast, there was the memorable First Bath. Medieval queens must have felt something like I did when they were expected to give birth to royal babies in public. Gingerly I sat on the edge of the tub while my daughters and husband stood by to help. They eased me into the water, holding the cast for dear life so it wouldn't get wet and melt.

Soon I gained sufficient confidence and graduated to the shower. Preparations were so elaborate they resembled an ancient purification and cleansing ceremony. I slipped a huge plastic bag over the cast, tied three white strips around the top end to keep out the drips, and donned a shower cap.

The next step was to get into the shower stall. How to do this? Backwards, naturally! I lifted myself on crutches up over the ledge and down into the shower, depositing crutches outside the door. Ritual completed, I turned on the shower and luxuriated in every drop.

After months of putting on all that stuff to bathe, I now feel downright *immodest* taking a shower without my equipment.

As all cast patients find out sooner or later, the area inside the cast is susceptible to itching. Much advice was given me on that score, and I tried it all.

There's the vacuum cleaner method, whereby you hold the nozzle of the hose to one end of the cast and try to blow the itch away. The trouble with this technique is that bends in the cast inhibit the flow of air.

Sprinkling bath powder into the cast was equally ineffective. It only adds to the accumulation of gook.

One intriguing suggestion was to drop coins down inside and periodically shake the leg. It rarely helped the scratching situation, but inadvertently led to my setting up a new banking system. Since coins rattled, I deposited bills. When the cast came off I had a total of $36.42. It didn't draw any interest, though, except from the nurse who cut off the cast.

Other suggestions were soda straws, sticks, rulers, fly swatters, and bent wire hangers. The hangers worked the best—at least from the top. I could poke around and scratch to my heart's content. If my foot itched I enlisted the assistance of whoever might be there to tackle that end. None of us, however, could get to the heel.

One remedy remained: Pretend it didn't itch. After eleven months of this I could relate to the chicken on that famous old cleansing powder ad which "hadn't scratched yet."

Some Applesauce for the Teacher

A good deal of my substitute teaching had to be cut back, and I was restless with not enough to occupy my mind. I missed being with high school kids. Therefore, when the opportunity came, I gladly accepted a short-term music assignment. As with the return to graduate school, I dreaded my first exposure to all those teenagers and their comments.

The young people proved me wrong. After a brief answer to "What happened?" and a demonstration of the famous Knee Hinge, class proceeded in near-normal manner. Except for a few saucy smart alecks who periodically took off with my crutches. Those wonderful kids didn't bring me apples, but honored me with a theme song every time I came into the classroom, "We Call Her Flipper."

Part of my assignment was to direct two choral groups at the Senior Baccalaureate service. One group sang on the speaker's platform. This simplified matters of movement for me. I was in position when the curtain opened, and I could get off unnoticed when it closed. But the second group was to sing from the rear balcony, up four stories. I had five minutes to get there.

The band director learned the music and prepared to man the battle station in the balcony in case I didn't make it in time. Three teachers waited in relay arrangement to help with music, crutches, and "Flipper." If I got going too fast, I might fall. One gentleman—indeed he was that—stayed in front of me so I could fall on him. Sir Walter Raleigh could have taken a few lessons.

I used to think a handicap horse race was one in which horses handicapped by sprained ankles, bad eyesight or similar disabilities had to race. To me that seemed positively cruel. Yet, here I was, racing to beat the clock. Beat it I did, and the kids performed beautifully.

Later that evening, I described all of this frantic activity to my husband. He laughed and hugged me to him, as close as the Interference would allow. He told me he was proud of me, and thought his filly deserved a suitable name for winning *her* Handicap.

"I love you, Hopalong Chastity," he whispered.

Those kids were what I've been needing, God. With all their teasing, their love came through with all the freshness and honesty of youth. I knew they were truly concerned about me, although they would rather be caught dead than admit it. I haven't laughed this much since before I fell down on the mountainside. God, thank You for all of them, even the ornery ones. They took my mind off myself and challenged the best in me to bring out the music that was in them. They helped clear up some "I" trouble.

But, most of all, I thank You for that man of mine who didn't know when he married me that he was in for such a rough time—long before any cast on my leg. He wants so much to trade places and carry this thing for awhile to give me rest from it.

He doesn't know that in many other ways he has been doing that. He has shared this "yoke" and we have grown together in a deeper love than we otherwise could have know. We had to learn the bad and the beautiful about each other. There were times when we were sure neither of us could bear any more.

We know more clearly now what Jesus meant when He, in effect, said, "Take My yoke upon you and the load will be lighter for each of us. And we shall learn ever so much about each other, 'cause

we're in this together." Isn't that what You want us
to learn when we share Your Yoke?
  I love that man of mine.
  I love You, Jesus.

The Show Must Go On!

Prearranged obligations do not anticipate accidents. When notations on my calendar reminded me several concerts were in the offing, my first impulse was to cancel them. My family took that decision out of my hands.

"Something creative would be good for you, Mom." The hint came through loud and clear. Mom was becoming a less-than-lovable person. In truth, a sour, old Grinch! Maybe I needed to sing more than anyone needed to hear me. Besides, I did not need my crutches now, and the idea became more and more appealing.

It took many days to get into voice again, and to plan and rehearse suitable programs. In addition, there was the careful consideration of what to wear. I needed a gown which would cover the cast and give room for all that structural engineering underneath. The dress I finally decided on did the latter. But, peeking out at the bottom, was that ugly white blob, revealing a set of ridiculously naked toes. It simply didn't go with sparkling earrings and a piled-up hairdo. So, out came my scissors, glue and scraps. A brief search turned up some suitable fabric. A few snips, some dabs of glue, and the result was a lovely new evening slipper and matching blob of gold brocade.

Getting on and off the stage without stumbling over members of the orchestra in a brand new walking cast also needed attention. I practiced endlessly, hoping to do so gracefully. It can't be done!

However, the show must go on. And, despite everything, the concert progressed smoothly—except for one little hitch.

In my excitement about singing again, I forgot to practice one small detail—bowing.

After the opening aria in my first A.C. concert, I automatically started to curtsy. I lifted the right leg to place it behind the left, as I always had and—got stuck! That was the leg with the cast on it! I couldn't go back and I couldn't bring it forward without falling on my nose! Only one thing to do—keep bowing, bending at my waist and bringing the top half of me down. I bobbed up and down (like after Halloween apples) half a dozen times.

But I had to get out of this mess before the applause died down—and it was thinning. I started to panic, so the next bob down, I turned my head in the direction of the conductor and yelled a whispered "Help!" Up I came and down again, as I turned in the direction of the concertmaster issuing another SOS! It worked!

Gallantly, and with perfect timing, the concertmaster stood up and took one hand as the conductor stepped off the podium and took the other. The audience exploded with applause and "bravos" as the three of us bowed again and again, and they escorted me offstage.

I'm not sure how well I sang, but the audience graciously called me back for several encores and more bows at the end of the concert. Looking back, I wonder if that was because of my singing, my

audacity under the circumstances, or if they wanted to see me get stuck again. I learned something, though. I sure know how to keep 'em clapping!

"O sing to the Lord a new song, for He has done wonderful things."

Thank You, God, for the gift of making music. It has powers of healing and is the universal language—another one of Your neat, beautiful creations. It opens up something inside of me, and like a bird, I can fly out of my cast-cage. I'm learning, too, that being deprived of one capacity sharpens and makes one appreciate all of Your other gifts. Make me always ready to share whatever gift You give me.

Knitting and Purling

In the wee hours one morning, I was disturbed by the sound of voices, intermingled with strange, clicking sounds. It startled me. I wanted to know where the voices were coming from. My children tell me I have excellent hearing when they are trying to keep something from me. It didn't take long to find out the noises were coming from inside my cast.

I sat up and leaned way over to find out what was going on. To my great delight, the bones were knitting fast and furiously.

Suddenly the clicking stopped, and there was a long silence.

"Hey, you, what's going on down there?" I asked the voices.

There was a pause, then a voice answered, "We're practicing our purling."

This really upset me. "What on earth are you doing purling when you should be knitting?"

Unaffected by my impatience, a voice went on to explain, "We've got the knitting down pat, but need some work on our purling."

I was mad. "Hey, you, I want to get out of this thing. Forget the purling, and tend to your knitting!" I shouted.

There was a gentle shake from my Bed Warmer. "Having a bad dream, dear?"

I mumbled something about their not knitting fast enough to suit me and went back to sleep.

During those waiting months, I tried knitting as a pastime, but gave it up. Somewhere along the line I had developed a mental block against purling. And, as any knitter knows, you can't make anything decent without it. As far as I'm concerned—purling is for oysters, and knitting should be strictly for bones—especially broken ones.

Thank You for the healing forces within my own body which You put there the moment I was conceived, God. Above all, let me have healthful, healing thoughts which bring together body, soul and spirit. But let me never lose sight of spiritual healing, so when this is over and You say "It is good," it will mean all of me, not just my bones.

Doctors

Doctors are a species unto themselves. They have to be, to put up with the assortment of patients and peculiarities. Doctors have to be positive, gentle, kind, capable, sympathetic and prophetic. They are expected to be healer, psychologist, counselor and miracle-worker. They're not supposed to get sick or die, since this would inconvenience those of us who call upon their skills.

Woe unto them if they fail to be any of these. Or keep us waiting too long. Or take Wednesdays off. Or charge too much. And many people think *anything* they charge is too much.

I'm sure that doctors, who are human, too, have a few bad apples in their barrel, but I have yet to meet one. On the other hand, I know many doctors who take care of patients who couldn't pay them a dime. And I know some who spend time on projects like the *USS Hope,* or trek into the hinterlands of primitive countries training medical personnel. Ministers, counselors, and other professional men often call upon them to help people with whom they are working. Time and again this help has been given without charge.

Most physicians don't know what a time clock is. Many rarely sleep a whole night through. As with other professional men, doctors are some of the loneliest people in the world. Their wives are lonelier still. Their medical and intellectual needs are constantly in conflict with their personal needs.

Doctors must also be actors. One especially good actor-doctor stopped by while I was in the hospital. I tried to wave him out since I was taking care of some pretty Basic Business. He didn't mind a bit, he said. But he sure left in a hurry.

I remember the kindness and thoughtfulness of many doctors during the early hours after my accident. Although they were not assigned to my case, they stopped in to chat and give encouragement. One of them, an ardent ski enthusiast, conveyed the utmost concern and wrongly blamed himself for not having given me some pointers before we went on our ski trip.

Enough cannot be said about my orthopedist, whose wise judgment and unruffled cool evidenced themselves when the chips were down. And boy, those chips were down. It took a genius to fasten them back in place.

Doctors' training is long and difficult. They have to take all kinds of classes. One course I think they all have to take is: "Strange Sounds to Make When You're Not Really Sure." They have to make sounds like UM, HM, UM HM, and UH HUH. Various shades, pitch and voice inflections can be used to give each sound a variety of meaning.

The word, *WELL,* is particularly important. It can convey all kinds of meanings, depending on how it is said. It takes years of practice to master all of its inherent potentialities.

Orthopedists have a special problem. Since the time for the repairing of bones varies widely between patients, they have to learn how to lengthen the sounds. I think the longer the sound the longer you're stuck with the old cast.

For example, UM becomes UMMMMM. HM—HMMMMM. UH HUH—UHHHH HUHHHH. UM HM—UMMMM HMMMM. The word, WELL, takes an awful beating. WWWWEEEELLLLLLLLLLLLLL!

Household Hints

In my miscellaneous drawer in the kitchen, there are lots of little papers and booklets offering helpful hints for maintaining a household. Believe me, in my state, they were quite useless. So I came up with a few of my own.

Getting something off a high shelf
Knock it down with your crutch.

When your crutch gets away from you
Get down on the floor and slide backwards to it. In addition, this provides good exercise.

Cooking
Use the Pivot System. Pivot on the good leg between refrigerator, sink and stove, while balancing lightly on the cast.

Setting the table
Let the kids do it.

Scrubbing the floor
I prefer the hands-and-knees method. It gets the floor cleaner, and has a humbling effect. But while "in the plaster," as New Zealanders say, sit on what you usually sit on and scrub around you. But, be prepared to explain why your pants are wet.

Driving

A broken *left* leg should not pose a problem. If it's the right one, however, learn to drive and brake with the left foot. Practice this deliberately at first. Take someone with you for moral support while you are learning, if you can find someone who is willing to go! (I checked the legality of this driving technique with the Highway Patrol. It does not matter which leg you use, as long as you are in complete control.)

Getting things from one place to another

If they are unbreakable, throw them. If you are

having a bad day, throw something breakable. It's
good therapy. Dirty clothes throw especially well. If
you miss your target, shove them with a crutch.
Regardless of how you may feel about crutches, they
can be useful.

Carrying stuff

Make an apron with little pockets, or borrow a
child's coloring apron, to carry little goodies. But be
careful about bending over when carrying sharp
things like pencils or scissors. It's better to have one
incapacity at a time. You'll find your neck becoming
handy for carrying things. Bath towels, dust rags,
eye-glasses on strings, and clothing can all be
transported in this manner. When the doorbell rings,
be sure to check what is hanging from your neck. I
forgot one time while gathering my lingerie to
launder.

Dressing

For women only. Since I don't know how men
dress, they will have to figure it out for themselves.
Put your dress on before you comb your hair. It's
easier to slip over the head than from below. As for
things that have to be put on from below: Either get
bigger sizes, or cut bigger holes.

How to help the budget

If you are going to break something it might be well
to consider a leg, since this can save a lot of stocking
or socks money. I used all my old single or pantyhose
this way. My teenage daughter's, too. She was happy
about this arrangement. I didn't make such a fuss

over the many pantyhose she ruined. I suppose this could apply to men and their son's socks.

For further hints, read chapters on Scratching, Showering, and Going Up and Down Stairs.

Eleven Month Miracle

The Day of Deliverance came. Silently my husband and I drove to the doctor's office, belying our keen anticipation. The nurse proceeded to cut into the iron-like plaster, section by section, with a vibrating machine which looked like a converted vacuum cleaner.

Gently she cut the cotton padding surrounding the leg, and I got my first look. It would not have won a beauty contest, but to me it was gorgeous. How I wanted to lift it. The last time I had attempted this without help of reinforcement, it had dangled limply. This time it stayed in one piece.

Doctor and Hubby carefully helped me into the car with my delicate prize. At home he and I bathed and examined the Masterpiece. But I could hardly wait until he left for the office. I wanted to be alone. There was something important I had to do.

Slowly I stood up, resting on the "good" leg. I grasped a chair, ever so carefully lifted my "new" leg, and swung it back and forth a few times. I set it down, and gradually shifted full weight to it. It held me up! I took a step, then another, and let go of the chair. I could walk, amazingly surefooted.

A Miracle had taken place. An eleven-month Miracle, but a Miracle nonetheless. ". . .Those who wait for the Lord will gain new strength." The doctor had done his work with marvelous skill. I had been a good patient. But there was a third Person who deserved recognition: The Great Physician who had created the "glue" which had stuck it all back together. He was there that day.

God, I can't say it. I can only feel it. You remember when You entered my hospital room and told me so vividly You would be delighted with each step I would take? Did You see me taking them? Maybe, God, You were also delighted with some of the other kinds

of steps You helped me with along this long path. Are
You as happy as I am? Are You delighted, God?

Yes, I think He was very delighted with His work. In fact, as I strutted back and forth, all the while thanking Him, I think I heard Him laugh out loud.

"I waited patiently for the Lord;
And He inclined to me, and heard my cry.
He brought me up out of the pit of destruction, out of
the miry clay;
And He set my feet upon a rock making my footsteps
firm.
And He put a new song in my mouth, a song of praise
to our God;
Many will see and fear,
And will trust in the Lord."
Psalm 40:1-3

Epilogue

To leave the impression that a badly broken leg and eleven months in a cast were a picnic would not be telling it like it is. As the weeks and months wore away, so did my spirits. I developed "castrophobia," and like a buried butterfly, wanted desperately to shed my cocoon. There were futile frustrations, tons of tears, and days of despair. I asked hundreds of times, "Will it ever end?"

To me the cast became an albatross, to the kids an overworked excuse for Mom to get out of housework, and to my husband an additional burden to the heavy pressures of his career. I love them all more dearly for putting up with me as well as they did.

It was through this year that I began to learn how to really pray. Not the catch-all, "God bless everybody," or "Hurry and heal me," or "Forgive me for my sins, if I have any." I learned *not* to pray, "Oh, Lord, I accept this punishment You inflicted on me to teach me a lesson"! Some Christians pray like that all their lives, and *really believe God is punishing them!* They cannot know my loving God! I learned these are all cop-outs. God knows what is eating us before we come to Him. We might as well be honest right off the bat, so we don't have to ask for more forgiveness.

Slowly I learned to trust His love enough to bear my deepest emotions, to dig out deeply buried resentments, and break cliche-ridden prayer habits.

Often I told God what I thought about Him and this whole mess—in no uncertain terms. In the process, awareness came of the games I was playing with Him and with others.

There were times when I experienced hysteria, and great anxiety about my physical healing. Gradually I came to a realization that another kind of healing was more urgently needed. In naked despair I learned to pray, "Okay, God, You take it from here. I'm tired of fighting."

It was what He had been waiting for. I gave Him my total broken empty self and will—an open channel. The corrosion and sludge which had been accumulating for years were cleaned out by the power of His Spirit. He moved into the deep recesses and crevices of my being like a laser, exposing all to His light. And a healing far greater than that of cellular tissue came.

There was a popular song a short time ago which began, "Walk a little slower when you walk with me." Although I can now walk as fast as before, I deliberately walk a little slower. There is a whole new dimension to life. I actually *see* the magnificent engineering of a flower. I hear pitches, colors, and vibratos in the singing of a bird that I had heard before, but to which I had not *listened*. I feel the closeness of people who pass by, and I feel as if we have sensed each other's gladness and caring.

I have new compassion for anyone on crutches, in a cast or wheelchair, or with a severe disability. I want to run up to them, love them, and tell them I understand.

Thus, a new world has come into my life. It begs me

to notice and give of myself to it. All because I "walk a little slower."

All this has had its effect on those around me. Recently my son saw a woman wearing a fresh new cast. After a moment's hesitation, he walked over to her, somewhat self-consciously. Then breaking into a reassuring grin he said, "My mom broke her leg, too. Don't get discouraged. She's getting along . . . JUST FINE!"

From the Bible

Sprinkled throughout this story of my experiences *Before Cast* and *After Cast* are references to something special in my Life Instructor's Guidebook—the Bible. Sometimes a full verse is quoted, sometimes just a pertinent snatch of a verse. Other times I put the thought in my own words—the Lucille Lavender version, tested and proved real to me. Here are those verses in full for you to read. May they bring help and solace to you, whatever may be your particular need this day.

Page 12
> "Pleasant words are a honeycomb,
> Sweet to the soul and healing to the bones."
> > Proverbs 16:24

Page 13
> "And he looked up and said, 'I see men, for I am seeing them like trees, walking about.' "
> > Mark 8:24

Page 16
> "O Lord, Thou hast searched me and known me.
> Thou dost know when I sit down and when I rise up;
> Thou dost understand my thought from afar.
> Thou dost scrutinize my path and my lying down,
> And art intimately acquainted with all my ways."
> > Psalm 139:1-1

Page 18
> "I will lift up my eyes to the mountains;

From whence shall my help come?
My help comes from the Lord,
Who made heaven and earth."
Psalm 121:1,2

Page 20
"Pride goes before destruction,
And a haughty spirit before stumbling."
Proverbs 16:18

Page 21
"For thus the Lord God, the Holy One of Israel, has said:
'In repentance and rest you shall be saved,
In quietness and trust is your strength.'"
Isaiah 30:15

Page 31
"Thy lovingkindness, O Lord, extends to the heavens,
Thy faithfulness reaches to the skies."
Psalm 36:5

Page 41
"I am poured out like water,
And all my bones are out of joint . . ."
Psalm 22:14

"I can count all my bones.
They look, they stare at me . . ."
Psalm 22:17

Page 42
"The steps of a man are established by the Lord;
And He delights in his way.
When he falls, he shall not be hurled headlong;
Because the Lord is the One who holds his hand."
Psalm 37:23,24

Page 55

"Why are you in despair, O my soul?
And why have you become disturbed within me?
Hope in God, for I shall yet praise Him,
The help of my countenance, and my God."
　　Psalm 42:11

Page 56

"When I consider Thy heavens, the work of Thy fingers,
The moon and the stars, which Thou hast ordained;
What is man, that Thou dost take thought of him?
And the son of man, that Thou dost care for him?
Yet Thou hast made him a little lower than God,
And dost crown him with glory and majesty!
Thou dost make him to rule over the works of Thy hands;
Thou hast put all things under his feet,
All sheep and oxen,
And also the beasts of the field,
The birds of the heavens, and the fish of the sea,
Whatever passes through the paths of the seas.
O Lord, our Lord,
How majestic is Thy name in all the earth!"
　　Psalm 8:3-9

Page 58

"I know how to get along with humble means, and I also know how to live in prosperity; in any and every circumstance I have learned the secret of being filled and going hungry, both of having abundance and suffering need. I can do all things through Him who strengthens me."
　　Philippians 4:12,13

Page 72

"Cast your burden upon the Lord, and He will sustain you;
He will never allow the righteous to be shaken."
　　Psalm 55:22

Page 76

"For God so loved the world, that He gave His only be-
gotten Son, that whoever believes in Him should not
perish, but have eternal life."

John 3:16

Page 79

[Jesus speaking] "'. . . Your heavenly Father knows that
you need all these things. But seek first His kingdom
and His righteousness; and all these things shall be
added to you. Therefore do not be anxious for tomorrow; for tomorrow will care for itself. Each day has
enough trouble of its own.'"

Matthew 6:32-34

Page 80

[Jesus speaking] "'. . . I was sick, and you visited Me; I was
in prison, and you came to Me.' And the King will answer
and say to them, 'Truly I say to you, to the extent that you
did it to one of these brothers of Mine, even the least of
them, you did it to Me.'"

Matthew 25:36,40

"Jesus said to him, 'Arise, take up your pallet, and walk.'"

John 5:8

Page 82

"Anxiety in the heart of a man weighs it down,
But a good word makes it glad."

Proverbs 12:25

Page 91

[Jesus speaking] "'. . . I came that they might have life,
and might have it abundantly.'"

John 10:10

Page 99

[Jesus speaking] "'Come to Me, all who are weary and heavy laden, and I will give you rest. Take My yoke upon you, and learn from Me, for I am gentle and humble in heart; and you shall find rest for your souls. For My yoke is easy, and My load is light."

Matthew 11:28-30

Page 105

"O sing to the Lord a new song,

For He has done wonderful things,

His right hand and His holy arm have gained the victory for Him."

Psalm 98:1

Page 106

"Behold, Thou dost desire truth in the innermost being,

And in the hidden part Thou wilt make me know wisdom.

Purify me with hyssop, and I shall be clean;

Wash me, and I shall be whiter than snow.

Make me to hear joy and gladness,

Let the bones which Thou hast broken rejoice.

Hide Thy face from my sins,

And blot out all my iniquities."

Psalm 51:6-9

Page 115

"Yet those who wait for the Lord

Will gain new strength;

They will mount up with wings like eagles,

They will run and not get tired,

They will walk and not become weary."

Isaiah 40:31